28 Days of Poetry Celebrating Black History 3

by Latorial Faison

Copyright © 2012 Latorial D. Faison

ALL RIGHTS RESERVED.

No part of this publication may be reproduced, stored in a retrieval system, or transmitted, in any form or by any means electronic, mechanical, photocopying, recording, or otherwise without the prior written permission of the author.

CROSS KEYS PRESS
crosskeyspress@aol.com

Printed in the U.S.A.

To Mama,
whose presence was priceless and
whose role in my life was
simply remarkable

Acknowledgements

I am thankful to *The Almighty* for giving me the *words* and *the will* to do this once again. In addition, there are those in the mundane who I owe gratitude as well. To my husband, who was overseas when this book was written, I am glad we have "A *Love.*" Thanks for being *my everything*. To our three sons, thanks for your enthusiasm and for *daily* challenging me in so many ways and on so many levels to fulfill *this* destiny that is *apparently* mine. I am proud to be *your* Mom. To Donna Bell and Ronika Herring, "*Ms. Donna and Ms. Ro,*" thanks for the first bulletin board "ever" in my honor. Your sincere response to my prior work was the catalyst for *this*, and there are absolutely *no words* to describe my gratitude for how you *unknowingly* poured into my spirit on all those Tuesdays and Thursdays. To Mr. Terrance A. Bell, "*Thank you*" and your wonderful wife for one of the best conversations I've ever had and for *your* writing of that marvelous article that went *national*. Last, but not least, to my FB family and friends, thanks for taking this journey with me. It *was* a February to remember *wasn't it?* Because of you, I *finished* this book. Thanks to those of you who "liked" or responded to each and every poem. I am *grateful*. To every teacher who invited me into the classroom and the countless, significant others of you reading, thank you. Remember *this* history. Celebrate *this* history, and pass *it* on. God bless you!

The most evil thing happened to the Black race here; it's called slavery.

Table of Contents

What is Black History?	11
He Preyed	13
The Trees on Their Backs	15
Fields of Praise	17
"For Sale"	19
Dreams of a Slave Woman	20
O Great Ancestor	22
The Fight	24
My Country, it was for Thee	25
Ruby Bridges' Brave Step *	26
What I Owe You	28
Obama*	32
The Black Vote	33
"The King of Pop" *	34
Whitney Houston: "The Voice" *	36
For a Songbird I Knew	38
A *Love*	41
Soul Food	44
Old Time Religion	45
There is So Much History *Here*	46
Nigger	48
I Could Scream a Negro Spiritual	49
A Dark Soliloquy	51
The *New* Slavery	55
If You See a Little Black Child	56
The Gist of It	59
Little Black Virginia Girl	61
Sankofa	63
Judgment Day	64
Legacy	66

Poems for Young Readers

What is Black History?

It is the dirt road our forefathers trod,
Memories of their lives branded in our hearts.
It is a word, a place, a state of mind.
Black history is a peek into our ancestors' time.

It is a piece of fabric our grandmothers wore,
An old rope that our grandfathers lived to deplore.
It is a slave ship and middle passage over seas.
Black history is cotton fields and tobacco leaves.

It is a plantation overseer and back door crumbs,
Weeping and wailing, a beating of drums.
It is a troubling truth, an unapologetic past.
Black history is an entire race struggling to last.

It is a Mississippi burning in a Tennessee town,
An evil that lingers to bring Black people down.
It is a book or movie of strength, courage, and will.
Black history is the fate of young Emmett Till.

It is little Ruby Bridges, the exquisite Ruby Dee,
Carter G. Woodson, and Coretta Scott King.
A Mahalia Jackson song, a Michael Jackson routine,
Black history is the phrase "Let freedom ring!"

It is Cheney University, the Tuskegee Airmen,
The N. A. A. C. P., the Black Holocaust Museum.
It is a navy master diver named Carl Brashear.
Black history is our legacy of triumph without fear.

It is General Colin Powell, a Vaudeville drama,
Zora Neale Hurston, and President Barack Obama.
It is every single experience of our history.
Black history is the story of you and me.

He Preyed

he preyed
this remarkable beast
this businessman from hell
who sought to
for a few
hundred years
waste God's time
enslaving a people

he watched
and waited
for young Africans
roaming prairies with pride
in their
motherland

then
he preyed
committing the great
abduction

he forced
matriarchs
to swim
in graves
beyond the deep
swallowing
waters
of pride
engulfed in
overtaken by
evil

he stole
bloodlines
and
sold them
for
lifetimes

he drove
patriarchs
to lives
of death
bound and chained
stripped of
manhood and wealth
mortified and defamed

this history
is impossible
to ascertain

yet
this beast
he so *remarkably*
preyed

The Trees On Their Backs

It's a valid question,
One we *all* should ask.
How exactly did they get
The trees on their backs?

They acquired these trees
For no good reason at all,
The reality of racial brutality
And the white man's laws.

The trees on their backs
Became emblems and signs
Of the demeaning experience
Known as slave times.

If they tried to escape
Or seemingly didn't work enough,
When mistresses were in a *tizzy*
Or masters felt like *bulking* up,

For the most insane reasons,
Slaves were whipped nearly to *death,*
Receiving *hundreds* of lashes
Until some took their last breath.

None enslaved were exempt
From the possibility of a tree.
Men, women, boys, or girls,
They couldn't escape it, you see.

They were whipped for simply looking
At *a* white person too long.
They were whipped for appearing
To be independent and strong.

They were whipped when suspected
Of learning how to read or write.
They were whipped just to *scare*
Every other slave in sight.

As you research Black history,
Be dedicated; pursue the facts.
Learn the truth concerning *everything*,
Even the symbolic *trees* on their backs.

Fields of Praise

with
their
backs
bent
they
picked
cotton
and
tobacco
leaves
sugar
cane
and
soy
beans
they
wore
little
and
labored
long
arranged
the
chorus
of
slavery's
song

they
dreamed
dreams
for
a
generation
craved
freedom
in
a
just
nation

they
bridged
a
gap
and
became
the
bridge
over
troubled
waters
that
we
have
lived

"For Sale"

From Zanzibar to Richmond
To be auctioned off and sold
Male and female negroes
Some young, some old

Carpenters and butlers
Laborers and field hands
Servants, cooks, and nurses
They were all in demand

Sold away from families
Sold far out of the state
Sold just like animals
Cruelty was their fate

Inspected and ostracized
Degraded and maligned
It was the true experience
Of the enslaved and confined

Dreams of a Slave Woman

She would stare into the distance
in search of a new dawning
that would bring freedom and justice,
hard work that produced a harvest.

She imagined a life of peace, not fear
or wondering when the master was near.
Her private parts, her inner parts, were more
than possessions; they were blessings.

Yet her womanhood was often misunderstood,
taken on the plantation, only to be awakened
to find herself disheveled, distraught and fraught
with rage after a raping.

Was she but black words on a colored page
in white women's books on a white man's stage?
Would she ever dream in color, live in harmony,
die in peace, bask in freedom?

Would she love exclusively, lie down and know
the man of her choosing? Donning chains of slavery,
her lot was bravery, to survive and recognize the
struggle, the cost of realizing a dream.

Could she keep her children, not have them sold south, underprivileged, bastard babies of miscegenation crying at the color of their skin, dying because of some unknown truth within.

She dreamed a slave woman's dream, tasted the sweetness of a slave woman's *freeing* . . . in her *mind*, *body,* and *soul*, it was a fight she dare not ignore, for *her* dreams were *to die for.*

O Great Ancestor

O great ancestor
who fought
for me
jumped
into the sea
to make a point
for me

O great ancestor
who stole away
for me
through swamps
and bad weather
enduring
tragedy
for me

O great ancestor
who lived
to love
me so
that horror
is all
you came
to know

O great ancestor
who realized rape
for me
endured
a test of fate
that I
might be

O great ancestor
who lost limbs and life
for me
lived plantation ills
for the future
of me

O great ancestor
who was hung and strung
from trees
in fear,
pain,
and agony
praying
to be
set free

O great ancestor
who was maimed
and killed
inhumanely held
against your will
who toiled
tired
in the field

O great ancestor
for your
sacrifice
this opportunity
this freedom
I owe you
my life

The Fight

You
may not
have seen the
civil rights
fight

But
it was
fought for you
just the
same

They
boycotted buses
so that you
could
fly

They
sat *in*
so that you
could eat
out

My Country it was for Thee

A King lived and breathed for thee
Taught Americans to stand up, be free

Gave insight to the spiritually blind for thee
What a monumental, costly legacy

A King organized marches and boycotts for thee
His crown was of faith, his message of peace

Robed in long-suffering and mere tranquility
His words were strength, courage, and humility

A King dreamed "the dream of dreams" you see
That you might overcome injustice, inequality

He sacrificed his life, gave it diligently
For a new day, America, he laid it down for *thee*

My country, it was for thee,
Sweet land so deliberately, of thee, *he'd* sing

Land where his fathers died,
Land where his children cried

From the inner cities to the country sides,
Let "The Dream" of the dreamer ring.

Ruby Bridges' Brave Step

The year was 1960
The day, November 14th
When a little Black girl
Was brave in New Orleans

Her name was Ruby Bridges
Some called her Ruby Nell
She lived through segregation
And gained quite a story to tell

William Frantz Elementary
Would never be the same
It was no longer a White school
The day that Ruby came

On her first day of school
She was so strong and proud
She stepped boldly without stopping
Through fiercely threatening crowds

There were people filled with hatred
Who told Ruby to go back home
They did not want integration
They taunted Ruby to make it known

But little Ruby had protection
Her mother, US Marshalls, and her God
As she stepped into this new school
Her teacher, Ms. Henry, won her heart

Ruby was, sometimes, afraid
But she prayed and continued on
With her family, teacher, and community
She weathered integration's storm

Ruby Bridges' experience
Is a significant part of history
Her unwavering faith and courage
Resulted in what we now see

Schools all across America
Integrated and diverse
Children of every color and creed
Learning together, breaking the curse.

What I Owe You

What I owe you Sir
what I owe you Ma'am
is what you gave
to me

You sat down
closed your weary eyes
thought of how
to make a way
for me

You didn't even
know my name
didn't know if I'd be
wild or tamed

But you
put your foot down
on a dusty road
took steps and bore
a heavy load
for me

To provide a future
less than poverty
you ate less, sleepless
breathed lifelessly
for me

You went barefoot
for me

Ploughed America's fields
for me

Ate leftovers
failed to look white folks
in their two eyes
for me

You sacrificed your dignity
thrived on a sad humility
for me

You took
slandering words and dirty looks
accusing stares
from devilish crooks
. . . for me

What I owe you
is what you gave

Therefore this road
is mine to pave

for the future

Lest our seed be
forgotten and lost

Lest our seed be
misguided, untaught

Lest our seed be
once again
for sale . . . then bought

The price is high
but we must
pay

Lest *this* history
repeat itself
today

Let me pay you
what I owe you
Sir

Let me give back
what you gave
Ma'am

For today
is all I
have

But tomorrow
is who I
am

Obama

Onward
believing
always in
miracles
America

The Black Vote

Don't take this right for granted;
It was not always there.
Today we have this right
Because our ancestors dared.

To take a stand, to stand in line,
To fight, and to even die,
We all have this right today,
But once we were denied.

The fight to vote was no easy task.
In fact, it was a challenging feat.
Blacks had to *first* be *citizens*
In order to compete.

They were real individuals
In a most cruel, unjust place,
But they had no rights at all
As people of the *Colored* race.

As you live in this democracy,
Enjoying every freedom of today,
Don't yield to platitudes of politics,
But vote for *those* who paved the way.

"The King of Pop"

On August twenty-ninth,
Nineteen fifty-eight
A most *talented* child was born;
Stardom would be his fate.

His parents named him Michael,
Michael Joseph Jackson,
An icon he'd live to become,
A musical genius and main attraction.

When Michael began his road to fame,
He was just a five-year-old boy.
He and his brothers, The Jackson 5,
Were childhood *wonders* to enjoy.

He became the group's lead singer,
Choreographer, and fashion guru,
But he ventured out, went solo,
His *own* musical dreams to pursue.

The little boy with the *powerful* voice
Became a *dancing machine* of a man,
Creating fads that fashion had never seen
Like a *sequined* glove on one hand.

Michael wrote, produced, and collaborated.
He directed, delivered, and *danced*.
The melodies and routines he brought to life
Left the world in *awe* and in trance.

He gave us albums like "Got to Be There,"
"Off the Wall," and "Thriller."
Jackson taught us that "We are the World,"
Made us *see* "The Man in the Mirror."

Michael was more than smooth.
His style was extraordinary and unique.
His perfected and popularized *moonwalk*
Gave way to lyrical ballads, profound and deep.

He's the most *famous* American artist,
The best entertainer of all time.
Setting Guinness world records,
He graced audiences with the *sublime*.

Michael Jackson's *incredible* voice,
His talent, and brilliance go un-topped;
Thus music fans the world over
Forever crown him the "King of Pop."

Whitney Houston: "The Voice"

It was the ninth of August,
Nineteen sixty-three
When Whitney Elizabeth Houston
Came here *to sing*.

Newark, New Jersey
Is where it all began.
She was destined for greatness,
And it *was* a Master plan.

Singing ran in Whitney's family;
Her vocal talent would take her far.
With family roots in the business,
She would become a *superstar*.

Whitney grew up singing gospel
In New Hope Baptist Church choirs.
Spiritually lifting congregations,
Her voice could take you *higher*.

In Whitney's early years,
She both modeled *and* sang.
She was the first Black female
To grace the cover of *Seventeen*.

Though Houston was a *natural* beauty,
Her career was not in fashion.
Instead, she'd become a national *treasure,*
With *the voice* that was everlasting.

When Arista records signed Houston
At the tender age of nineteen,
It was only the beginning
Of the ballads that she would sing.

Whitney's first album topped every chart
Winning her a Grammy Award in 1986.
She was an overnight sensation,
A cross-over with range, she was *it*

From *The Bodyguard* to *The Preacher's Wife*,
Whitney's talent never held back.
She wowed movie-goers and music lovers
With *hit singles* and amazing *soundtracks*.

Hers was a *transcending* talent for all times;
She *was* "the voice" of her generation.
Whitney Houston was a *life* in song,
A testament of courage and inspiration.

For a Songbird I Knew

You
supernatural
mezzo-soprano
beautiful, dynamic,
reassuring and enduring,
beautiful sound

the voice

Princess
of soul
of soulful ballads
music, lyrics,
and love
made from
melodies, octaves
melodramatic sureties

You
Whitney *you*
imbued
what is beautiful
what is rare
what is blessed
what is *talent*

Trumpets
and flutes
pianos and organic
blues wooed our ears
through a generation of
musically empowered years
elevated us to other
stations and stature

You
took listeners
to the simply *rational*
brought us from disaster
with your truth
your love ballads

Naked
you appeared
not bewildered
but secured
in the fire of your flames
the utter *charisma*
of your name

It
was not
a superstar's game
you played
it was your life

I
ain't mad at you
just blessed that you
came to play
never to stay
but to brighten up
an ordinary
day

with music
with laughter
with love
with joy
with *the voice*

You
Whitney *you*
live on, dream on
love on, sing on
up there

For
down here
there's a beauty now
there's a blessing now
there's a memory now
a reflection now
of *you*

Silhouettes
and soulfulness
a daring
sometimes *domineering*
songstress
who fought the fight of
reality laced in *duality*
carnality *in search of*
spirituality

You
left us without
really leaving us

For
we will *always*
have you
as long as we have

"the voice"

A *Love*

This
is a *love* poem
and I'm writing it
like Whitney
would sing it

In mezzo-soprano
with *highs* and *lows*
filling hearts and souls

Men and women
ladies and gentlemen
"Let's stay . . . together!"

In love, let's be a lyric
paint the sky red and
fly rockets to bed

Let's melt into a melody
hang from cliffs in climax
screaming scats in pure
ecstasy

I told you
this . . . is a love poem
so you've been warned

Let's be a long
strong ballad
get lost in
baby-making sighs
the soft echoes
of love cries

Let's be betrothed
synchronize our heartbeats
get baptized
emerge as two souls
one feat

Let's sit on the rock
and feel *God*
receive *His* blessing
flow in *His* anointing
read *His* handwriting
on our walls

Let's pray
for a more *perfect* union
that we might
rule *together*
enjoy dominion
forever

I can be
God's Eve *corrected*
you can be
His Adam *redirected*
together we can be
love *perfected*

In *love*, about *love*, all for *love*
to love beyond love and above love
me for you and you for me
for that's the kind of love
our love *should* be

A *His* kind of love
an *our* kind of love
Etta's "Saturday kind of love"
when "your love is my love"
and our love is
His love

It's a love, it's a *love*
always will be . . .
a love

Soul Food

slave living
mixed
with African
traditions
offered up
southern cuisines
combined with
unique
recipes from
plantation
scraps and
leftovers that
left eating
to the
creative
the resourceful
the remnant
of an
ancient
civilization
for survival
nutrition
and the
establishment
of new traditions
this gift
came to us
on greens
of collards
the black eyes
of peas
lard
and salty
hocks
of hams
delicious
fruit cobblers
sweet potatoes
and jams

Old Time Religion

In our Sunday best we ate chicken, rolls, and potato salads,
attended Easter skits, Christmas plays, and spring rallies.

Choirs marched down aisles singing "Glory to His name,"
and from *Amen* corners a few dignified deacons came.

As church mothers taught us at Sunday school,
from an old coffee can we got to choose

Our favorite crayon with which to color Christ
walking on the water or giving new life.

Trustees cleaned and filled the pool outside
for many lost souls who would be revived.

Men, women, and children, they all were brave
if they came to the mourners bench to be *saved*.

From the Good Book, reverends *charismatically* read,
proclaiming that "for our sins the Savior bled."

Spirits were bound, loosed, and lifted,
and the people of God were *slain* in the Spirit.

There is So Much History *Here*

This is where most
if not all of it
began

here . . . with me, with you
my mother, your mother
your father, my father
their mothers, their fathers

somewhere in an African bush,
slave castles, or the remnants of Cush

it happened

captured
   taken
inhumanely mistaken
     genocide and *raping*
of a people

who now live with a mixture of
   blood
     memories
       feelings
successful and unsuccessful
attempts at *freedom* and *healing*

there is no mystery
in the *middle passage*
just the reality
of blood and ashes
strewn about an
American south

wake up
the fighters for freedom

shake up
the molders of democracy

reach up
from hands of hypocrisy

for there is *so much* history
here

Nigger

Never call a soul *this*, outside any given name,

Igniting racial tension, displaying ignorance and shame.

Grab hold of this word's *history*, and visualize its *stain*.

Gather intellectual enlightenment, help to *heal* the pain.

Erase *this* disrespectful word, its derogatory existence,

Reflecting *only* on its past use and historical significance.

I Could Scream a Negro Spiritual

I could scream
a *Negro* spiritual
but you would not
hear

I could raise
red flags
sewn by hands of
the downtrodden
the forgotten
but you would not
notice

I could pray
the prayer of salvation
cast out demons
rid you of abominations
but you would not
be saved

I could laugh
like Achebe's
"beautyful ones"
but you would not
smile

I could cry
red rivers
of Jim Crow towns
but you would not
feel me

I could summon
God
in trinity
but you would not
believe

A Dark Soliloquy

How long? Too long.

I have watched my people
come to ruins, undo a generation
with immorality and spiritual degradation

Young children look on
with no hope as they look on
at parents using and abusing dope
using and abusing *them*

Have we truly cried *for us*
because they truly died *for us*
and we can't seem to get ahead *for us*

For us, for us . . . *for us*!
the time is not now for us
it was yesterday

We needed to be awakened *yesterday*
we needed to love *yesterday*
we needed to be educated *yesterday*
we needed to be motivated *yesterday*

We needed to invest *yesterday*
we needed to be married *yesterday*
we needed a job *yesterday*
we needed a place to call our own *yesterday*
we needed salvation . . . *yesterday*

Today I hum and pen a Black girl song
and listen to Black boy beats
as too many Black babies are lost
to the streets
city streets, country roads
for this tragedy, this chaos
did the great pavers carry this load?

Why are we so ungrateful?
Why stand we in positions unshakeable,
unmoved by these masses of ignorance
the mass production of indolence
the audacity of complacency ... *not hope?*

I can't cope
you can't cope
little boys and girls
cannot *cope*
with this uncertainty
this counter-productive bureaucracy
this b.s. . . . this b.s. . . . this *BS!*

Have we no shame?
Have we any morals?
Have we any love?
Have we any religion?
Have we any *common sense?*

Today's preachers are preaching wealth
instead of waiting for the promise
because Heaven can't seem to wait ... *for us*
Black man ... GOD can't wait for us
to change, to know better, to *do better*

To stop the rape of babies
the utter disregard and disrespect for ladies
no place for a Black queen in the Black community
she renounces her thrown *today*
to lies, to prostitution, to confusion,
to child neglect, to abusing ... *the system*

If I had a dollar
for every one of us who stood
with too much surety
on this system of nothing-but-*handouts*
I would be rich, I could scratch a seriously annoying *itch*
for my people, for the children, for the lost

Our paradise
is *lost* . . .

Black Adam left Black Eve
because he didn't like
her fruits, her needs,
what together they could
conceive and achieve

Black Adam left Black Eve
because he could not
believe

And now Black Eve
can't seem to succeed
without the notion
that she *too*
has been deceived

Giving too much
of *nothing*
without living too much
for *nothing*
neglecting her seed
for *nothing*
without *nothing*
and from *nothing*
she leaves
NOTHING!

The garden has been
more than rearranged
it's gone
it's been forgotten
a memory, a place, a chapter
in a book called *Genesis*
a book we fail to read
or come to anymore
for the creed
on how to get life *right*

For *we*
have been duped

We believe
that power is in people
not God

We believe
that power is in places
not God

We believe
that power no longer
grows within but *without*
us

The power is
without us

Without *us*
is the power
of *us*

The *New* Slavery

Our struggle is
No longer physical
Our conflict
All the more complex

Our issue is no more
With the white man
It rests now with a new
Lone suspect

The single greatest enemy
That we battle today
Is the inner man inside
Disillusionment and dismay

Some of us have lost courage
Others have lost the way
Many have grown disheartened
Too many *fail* to seize the day

The shackles of our ancestors
Are still fixtures in our lives
Not binding up our hands and feet
But now entangling our minds

We endured a *tragic* history here
The white man gave us hell
But in this new millennium
We now lynch *ourselves*

If You See a Little Black Child

I saw a little black girl
trying to be white
she tried and tried
with all her might

She straightened her hair
and colored her eyes
she bleached her skin
and lived white lies

I saw a little black boy
trying to do the same
loved to hear the white girls
just calling his name

He worked awful hard
to find his place
but when he found it
he gave it to a white face

If you see a little black
girl trying to be white
remind her of
her ancestors' plight

Tell her stories
about the old South
where Black mother and child
were both sold out

If you see a little black boy
trying to do the same
tell him of the history
from whence he came

Tell him shocking stories
of the old slave trade
how white folks claimed
a *nigger* was made

If you see a little black child
trying to be white
tell her about Black women
their courage and might

So that she may know
her own self worth
that she was predestined for greatness
at her birth

If you see a little black child
trying to be white
tell him about Black men
their pride and fight

So that he, too, may know
about his history
that he was born to provide,
to lead his family

The Gist of It

Let's get to
the gist of it
we now stand in
the midst of it

What they did
back in history
today there is
no mystery

Look to your left
look to your right
we are a people
out of sight

We were
given nothing
to prove
something

At the end of
each and every rope
we held on
to life and hope

So many steps
so many strides
too many sacrifices
too many lives

They sang
they preached
they danced
they leaped

They stood
they fought
they marched
they taught

We were a people
proud and strong
we were a culture
enduring on

And that's about
the gist of it
we now stand in
the midst of it

Little Black Virginia Girl

I am a black woman
Who shall *never* forget
For the color of my skin
Is now part of my wit

Some say that *I*
Need to let the past go
But if they wore my shoes
Then they would know

See, you can erase words
But memories, you never can
I grew up gifted and black
But under a Jim Crow plan

Not separate, just *unequal*
Everywhere I turned
As a little black Virginia girl
It was what I learned

For eight hours of the day
We mingled and mixed
But certain things in life
Were for all *white* cliques

I had to excel even further
Achieve above and *beyond*
For a license to fish
In the white man's pond

They say life has *changed*
Yet it's *somewhat* the same
For all the little Black children
Forced to play this game

Sankofa

Your past is
your history
the truth telling
mystery
of you

Go back
and get it

Any start
without it
is *false*

Any thing
and everything
you start
begins with *it*

It's never wrong
to reach back
for revelation
to go back for
the forgotten
the truth

Judgment Day

When
that day
comes

When
tables
turn

When
color is
erased

We'll
descend
this mountain
of hypocrisy

We'll
seek a saving
grace

There
will be no
black

There
will be no
white

Only
truth and inner
light

Abandoned
racism and
segregation

Discarded
bigotry and
discrimination

Farewell
to fathers who
founded thee

All who failed
to make *this*
freedom free

The Legacy

To each and every
    Black achiever
My goal has been
    To make you a believer

Believe in yourself
    Believe in your vision
Believe in your history
    Believe in wisdom

You are capable
    You are bright
You are strong
    So full of light

Be dedicated, educated
    Steadfast, firm believers
Above all, strive to continue
    The legacy of Black achievers

28 Days of Poetry
Celebrating
Black History
Volume 3

Book a Poet for Your Next Event!

Poetry Readings & Book Signings
Writing Workshops
Festivals, Conferences, Graduations
Black History & Women's History Months
National Poetry Month
Reading & Literacy Awareness
Community Events
Churches, Colleges & Universities

To schedule an event with Faison, email
crosskeyspress@aol.com

Purchase books by Faison at Amazon.com

Visit Latorial Faison's Official Website
www.latorialfaison.com

Made in United States
Orlando, FL
21 February 2023

30252956R00039